Step-by-Step Transformations

Turning Cotton into Clothes

Amy Hayes

Cavendish Square

New York

Published in 2016 by Cavendish Square Publishing, LLC
243 5th Avenue, Suite 136, New York, NY 10016

Library of Congress Cataloging-in-Publication Data

Hayes, Amy.
Turning cotton into clothes / Amy Hayes.
pages cm. — (Step-by-step transformations)
Includes index.
ISBN 978-1-50260-449-1 (hardcover) ISBN 978-1-50260-448-4 (paperback) ISBN 978-1-50260-450-7 (ebook)
1. Cotton—Juvenile literature. 2. Cotton manufacture—Juvenile literature. I. Title.

TS1575.H39 2016
677'.2164—dc23

2014049481

Editorial Director: David McNamara
Copy Editor: Cynthia Roby
Art Director: Jeffrey Talbot
Designer: Alan Sliwinski
Senior Production Manager: Jennifer Ryder-Talbot
Production Editor: Renni Johnson

Printed in the United States of America

Contents

Clothes are made from cotton.

4

Cotton is a plant.

First, cotton is picked in a cotton field.

Next, the cotton is brought to the factory and cleaned.

9

The combing machine turns the cotton into **sliver**.

11

The sliver is stretched thin and spun together.

It is now **roving**.

13

Next, the roving gets
stretched again.

It is now **thread**.

15

All these threads are put together in a **loom**.

16

17

The threads are **weaved** together to make cloth.

Then it is cut.

18

19

Finally, the cut cloth is sewed together.

It is now clothing!

21

New Words

loom (LOOM) A machine that weaves threads together to make cloth.

roving (ROH-ving) A slightly twisted strand of fibers.

sliver (SLIH-ver) An untwisted strand of fibers.

thread (THRED) A thin, fine cord.

weave (WEEV) To form interlacing strands into cloth.

22

Index

23

About the Author

Amy Hayes lives in the beautiful city of Buffalo, New York. She has written several books for children, including the Machines that Work and the Our Holidays series for Cavendish Square.

About BOOK WORMS

Bookworms help independent readers gain reading confidence through high-frequency words, simple sentences, and strong picture/text support. Each book explores a concept that helps children relate what they read to the world in which they live.